A Pub On Every Corner

Volume Two: South Liverpool

Freddy O'Connor

THE BLUECOAT PRESS

I would like to acknowledge the following
for their help with research and material:

Liverpool Records Office
Crosby Library
Lancashire Records Office
City Magistrates Licensing Section
Garston Old Comrades Club
Bryn Jones, Arthur Mitchell,
Ted Senar, Ted Williams,
Gerry Woods

Special thanks to my wife Jean, my Dad,
my brother Frank and John McKeown.

*Pubs listed in any given era that are classed as "not
listed" means that they were either closed or
demolished, or in a few instances may have reopened
at a later date either as a public house or diffferent
business, whereas pubs listed in 1964 or 1970 were
all open in those years, but since demolished.
Certain pubs list the licensee and registered owner
from 1892, this is to feature the diversity of over a
century ago.*

Abbreviations:
BH – Beer House
PH – Public House
WSV – Wine & Spirit Vaults

© Freddy O'Connor 1997

Published by the Bluecoat Press
Bluecoat Chambers
Liverpool L1 3BX

ISBN 1 872568 38 6

Design: Pencilpoint
Origination: Primary Four
Print: G.Z. Printek

Toxteth & Dingle

PRINCES ROAD, 1921

In the late 18th century, Toxteth Park was mainly rural. As late as 1790, only four houses stood on Parliament Street, which was previously named Towns End Lane - the boundary of Liverpool and Toxteth Park. Toxteth Park was a royal park created by King John about the time Liverpool was founded. It is hard to imagine wild boar and deer once roamed amongst the trees and valleys of the park. In the early years of the 17th century, Toxteth was disparked and, in 1640, came into the ownership of the Earl of Sefton. In 1775, after an Act of Parliament, the land was gradually built upon with the intention of it becoming a town named Harrington. This name, however, was rarely used and, although still officially Toxteth Park, this name too fell into disuse. After incorporation into Liverpool in 1836, the area became known as Dingle. In 1895, Toxteth was fully absorbed into Liverpool. Since the early 1980's, the name Toxteth has been reintroduced.

Sadly, the hideous slums of Liverpool 1 were extended into Liverpool 8. However, from the 1860's, court property ceased to be built and the construction of uniform terraced streets continued southward. Congested slums were mainly confined to beyond the old boundary, in the area bounded by Parliament Street southerly, along St. James Place and Park Place and then to the west down Warwick Street to the Dock Road (Sefton Street) and back to Parliament Street. In common with the teeming slums of other areas, numerous pubs stood in this vicinity although, like the slums, the majority of the pubs have been demolished.

managed by Michael Carberry, it was the last pub of 14 in the street and was demolished in the 1980's.

Brunswick Hotel

This view of the pub on Sefton Street features a way of life that is now just a memory; dockers waiting in the rain in the hope of being picked for work. No doubt some of the ones turned away would go straight into the pub if they had enough money for a pint. Before closure the pub was locally known as the 'Seven Steps'. The premises have since been refurbished and reopened as another business.

The continuation of Parliament Street at St James Street is Upper Parliament Street. Although significantly longer than the former, it only contained 9 pubs. (Parliament Street is some 498 yards long compared to just over 1 mile for Upper Parliament Street). The street had so few pubs because it was built for the town's merchants and more affluent townsfolk who, like their modern counterparts in the suburban areas of south Liverpool, did not place pubs high on their list of priorities.

The following are/were in Liverpool 8:

Californian Vaults

On Parliament Street at its junction with Dwerryhouse Street, its site has been replaced by industrial premises. Photographed in the 1920's when

Queens Vaults

The pub stood at the corner of Upper Parliament Street and Crown Street and was demolished in the early 1970's. In 1993, the vicinity was cleared of houses that were only twenty years old for the construction of a new women's hospital that opened 1995 and replaced three hospitals - Mill Road (already demolished), Oxford Street and the Women's, Catharine Street.

Alexandra

Standing at the junction of Upper Parliament Street with Oliver Street (abolished), it appears to have been

built as an extension of a large house. The pub, photographed here c1960 when the manager was Peter Condon, was known locally as the 'Mad House' and demolished in the 1970's.
1892 Licensee: Robert Teggin. Registered Owner: P. Walker & Son, Brewer

Stanley Arms

Located at the lower end of the street at the junction with Rathbone Street, the premises were demolished during the widening of the street in the 1980's. The name of the street can be seen on the glass of the gas lamp. Photographed c1912, the pub was known as 'The Scalers' after men working as scalers on the docks who frequented the pub. A Police Report of 1898 recorded that 'the husband of the licensee holds the license for the public house 89 Mill Street. The back door of the free lending library next door opens into the yard of the public house and when the door of the yard is locked the police have no access.' A Police Report from 1903 noted: 'Selling drink to a drunken man; ten shillings and costs.'

Clevedon Arms

Listed at Upper Parliament Street at its junction with Embledon Street. As can be seen from this

photograph the old housing on either side of the pub has long been demolished and the surrounding area recently landscaped. At the time of writing the premises, known locally as the 'Glue Pot', remain closed.

1892 Licensee: James R. Henderson. Registered Owner: P. Walker & Son.

From the 1950's Upper Parliament Street and its vicinity housed most of Liverpool's night clubs outside of the city centre, including many illicit drinking dens frequented by foreign seamen. Similar to the old beer houses, they were often just a front parlour of a dwelling house. An amusing incident concerning one such club was related to me by a friend. In the 1950's, Custom and Excise decided to raid a club via the roof. However, the owner was aware of the raid and, as soon as the officials were on the roof, the ladder was removed. By the time the red faced officials were rescued, the house was completely "dry".

Many readers will have their own memories of frequenting such clubs including the following on Upper Parliament Street :

Silver Swallow Social Club (number 4); All Nations Club (Lucky Bar) (15a); Tudor Club (Dutch Eddie's) (60); Nigerian Social Club (64); Jamaica House (142); Beacon Social Club (144); Yoruba Social Club (200) Granby Labour & Social Club (252); Granby Conservative Club (318); and the Olympus, Alahram, Gladray and Somali clubs.

The Rialto Building, at the junction of Upper Parliament Street and Berkley Street, was a former well known landmark destroyed in 1981. Its last use was as a furniture business, prior to which it housed shops (including a WSM) and a cinema which closed in 1964. It is fondly remembered for its ballroom which closed in 1965. A new Rialto Centre housing shops, offices and flats has just opened in the same location.

Although the above-named clubs thrived in the 1950's and 1960's, it appears that the 1930's was a more notorious decade, as the following Police report states: 'Between the world wars and particularly the Thirties, the borough police became alarmed by the spread of slum clubs. Many, they discovered, were structurally unsound, insanitary, and were run by bookmakers, solely for drinking and betting. They became notorious for the excessive drinking, foul language and the grossest obscenities practised in them between men and women. For many years, the constables had great trouble in curbing their menace because they were easily registered and opened and usually introduced elaborate precautions such as spy holes, electric bell warning systems, barbed wire and heavy iron doors to keep out the police.'

The interior of the Racquet Club (c1947)

One of many exclusive members clubs that thrived when class distinction was still blatant. Founded in 1877, it had its heyday when Upper Parliament Street was an affluent residential area.

The peak of licensed clubs in Liverpool was in the 1960's when there were 242 licensed clubs. A change

in the law concerning gambling had swelled the number, many of which were licensed gambling clubs. The huge popularity of gambling in the 1960's can be illustrated well by betting shops; illegal before 1961, an incredible 507 were trading by 1965.

Peter Kavanagh's.

Open to date at 2 Egerton Street off Catharine Street, north of Upper Parliament Street. Although northward from this point is Liverpool 7, some streets such as this one were/are in Liverpool 8 due to the original irregular boundaries. Pre-1890's the premises were named The Liver. In the late 1890's the premises were taken over by Peter Kavanagh and became named The Grapes.

Peter Kavanagh became a well known victualler of Liverpool, remaining at the pub until his death in 1950. He was also a long serving Councillor and was credited with a number of inventions, including a twist-lock table that was fitted to the floor, a very

Comet Vaults (bottom left)

This large imposing structure was at the junction with Ashwell Street. The pub survived until the late-1970's before demolition. The photograph is from the 1890's with a British Workman Public House adjoining.

Ye Olde Tally Ho

Listed at 45 St James Place and displaying its name on the window. Note a court entrance (court number 3) flanked with iron railings next to the pub. The pub closed in 1915. The advertisement on the wall was advertising property for sale, whilst the Daily Dispatch poster reads: 'Liverpool Ship Sinks In Mid Atlantic: Sailors' Week Of Peril'. The licensee was Henry H. Thomas when photographed c1908. An 1892 Police report states: 'Supplying drink to a police constable whilst on duty. Dismissed.'

useful contraption for passenger liners, which adopted the idea. The pub gradually became known as simply Peter's, or Peter Kavanagh's and, in fact, was so named by the 1930's, as this view indicates. During the 1950's the premises still remained in the family listed to Percy Kavanagh.

At the southern foot of Upper Parliament Street is St James Place, now part of a widened thoroughfare as the continuation of Great George Street with practically nothing remaining on its frontage. It contained 10 pubs, none of which remain.

COMET VAULTS

As the docks and dock-related industries began to flourish in the district, Stanhope Street and later Upper Stanhope Street became built-up with slum housing, court property, industrial premises and pubs. Stanhope Street also contained a number of breweries, one listed as early as 1805. A brewery that has survived to date is Cain's. The name "Stanhope" derives from the marriage of the first Earl of Sefton to Isabella Stanhope, the daughter of the Earl of Harrington. In all, 24 pubs were listed on Stanhope Street.

Coburg Hotel

Listed at the corner of Stanhope Street and Sefton Street, the pub is open to date. This view is from the 1920's when the manager was Thomas Llewellyn

Angel

Open to date on the corner of Stanhope Street and Caryl Street. The terraced property shown on either side of the pub has long been demolished and replaced by industrial units. Photographed in 1904 when the licensee was Edward Caveney.
1892 Licensee: James Charnley. Registered Owner: Robert Cain, Brewer

Old House at Home

Listed at 46 Stanhope Street and one of the street's long-closed pubs, the licence having expired as long ago as 1911. Photographed in the 1890's when the

Matthews. For many years the pub has been known locally as the 'Devils'.

Strangely, the pub was named the 'Devils' for one year only, in 1890. Apparently, there was a sideboard in the bar that had the head of a devil which was illuminated from behind, giving a real devilish effect. The sign that hung outside was also in the guise of the devil. During the 1840's, the pub was listed as 142 Stanhope Street (renumbered 1 -3 by the 1850's) and was named the Transatlantic Hotel. It had another name change, for one year only in 1880, when re-named the 'Tam O Shanter'. The pub was then named the Coburg from the 1890's to date. The pub contains a list showing the names of all the former managers.

manager was James Mackie. By the 1920's, the building had become a shop. Note the old advertisements on William Colquitt's adjoining tobacconist shop and Eleanor White's chandler's which include Hudsons Soap, Watsons Matchless Cleaner, Sporting Chronicle and Athletic News. A police report of 1892 recorded that the 'back door opens into enclosed entry, into which the back doors of seven private houses lead. When the gate at the end of the entry is closed the police have no access to the back door of the public house.'

Bishop

The Bishop stood on the corner of Stanhope Street and Beaufort Street and was originally surrounded by

loathsome court property. Photographed c1960 when the manager was Albert Harwood and the vicinity was in the process of demolition.

Prince of Wales

One of the older pubs in Stanhope Street. An old worn out board on the pub advertises the pub's earlier name, the Standard of which the first three letters can still be seen along with "HB" (referring to Henry Brooks, licensee when photographed in the 1890's). Pre-1860's, the pub was named the Havelock). The pub had closed by the 1920's and was trading as a shop soon after. The adjoining premises (74 Stanhope Street) was one of the streets brewer's, Clegg & Wright, who were taken over by Peter Walker's in 1901.

Police report (1892) 'Selling drink to a drunken man.

Dismissed. Also selling drink to a child under 14. Dismissed.'

1892 Licensee: Henry Brooks. Registered Owner: Mr Ellis (Pawnbroker of Great George Place)

Stanhope Street continues eastward to Upper Stanhope Street which once contained 10 PHs.

Princes Park Hotel

Listed at 118 Upper Stanhope Street at the junction with Carter Street. A large corner local, known

locally as Sadie's, this photograph from the 1970's shows an adjoining restaurant - the New Moon. The pub was demolished in the early 1980's; its site and adjoining land is still derelict.

Upper Stanhope Street

The large number of pubs in the vicinity reflected the densely populated area, with court property in

abundance. The squalid conditions that existed in streets such as Upper Stanhope Street were to take many years to eradicate. This is number 3 court, photographed in the 1930's. During the 1960's, such property was finally eliminated from the city.

Running eastward from the river parallel to Stanhope Street and Upper Stanhope Street is Hill Street and Upper Hill Street. Both contained similar poverty-stricken courts amidst the ever-present public houses. Hill Street contained some 20 pubs (two listed in 1820's) with 13 in Upper Hill Street.

Highland Home Hotel

Still trading at 6/8 Hill Street. Although currently in use as a hotel, the two buildings in this photograph were separate premises pre-1960's, with the smaller building listed as Threlfalls Dining Rooms from the 1920's to the 1950's (prior to which the premises had various uses including a tobacconist and eating house).

The Highland Home was so-named by the 1850's, replacing an earlier PH named the Pilot Boat. It changed its name to the Model Vaults in the 1860's but had restored its current name during the1890's. The faded sign for Threlfall's Ales can still be seen on the gable end.

Dick Jennings

Still trading on the corner of Hill Street and Mill Street, currently standing in isolation. Named after a former manager Dick Jennings (Richard Jennings, the manager in the 1940's and 50's), it was previously

named the Woods House and, pre-1930's, the Grapes. This 1920's photograph shows working-class men in typical attire of the day, standing around outside the pub with the name of the street displayed on the gas light.

Weathercock

Photographed in the 1970's, the Weathercock stood at 117 Hill Street at its junction with Mill Street. Although the pub shown replaced an earlier building, the premises closed and were demolished in 1990.

Grecian Hotel

The Grecian, locally known as the 'Snake Pit', stood at the junction of Upper Hill Street and Berkley

Street. This view from the 1980's shows the pub standing derelict and in isolation. In the background, the demolition of high-rise flats is in progress. The pub itself remained standing for a further few years until demolition.

Alexandra

Upper Hill Street has been physically "broken up" since the 1960's. The Alexandra is open to date near the upper limit of the street at its junction with Gibson Street. The view is from the 1920's when managed by John Airey. Adjoining the premises on Gibson Street was Owen Eames' joinery, whilst the premises on Upper Hill Street was listed to Thomas Maclese & Co., motor engineers and is still in use as a garage to date.

A typical court, 1920

A little further south from Hill Street running eastward from the Dock Road is Warwick Street which once contained 12 public houses.

Warwick Castle

This pub at the corner of Warwick Street and Wolfe Street was in the midst of one of the towns worst slum areas. To the left is Wolfe Street and on the other side of the pub is New Henderson Street (Henderson Street pre-1890's).

An 1883 report entitled 'Squalid Liverpool' stated that 'its worst streets are Wolfe Street, Henderson Street and Mann Street. The latter is perhaps the most persistently unhealthy street in Liverpool, for no year has passed since 1865 in which deaths in it have not been recorded from fever. In 1882 eleven deaths were officially notified. Henderson Street has been free from fatal cases for only three years out of the period referred to, Wolfe Street for four. There are about 160 houses in Henderson Street and 25 inhabited courts on an average of four houses each. At a very moderate estimate you may allow seven persons for each house and supposing each to be occupied - which fortunately is not the case at present - you would have in this street alone a squalid population of at least 1,800 persons.'

Despite this report, where it mentions 25 inhabited courts in Henderson Street, some 40 years earlier the street contained an incredible 45 courts on its length of 402 yards. Wolfe Street, which was 405 yards long, contained 10 courts and 11 public houses.

The continuation of Warwick Street eastward is Upper Warwick Street which contained seven public houses.

Royal Oak

The Royal Oak, on the corner of Upper Warwick Street and Park Place is the only pub remaining on the street. The pub, replacing an earlier one, opened in 1958 to serve the tenements of Sussex Gardens built in the early 1950's.

BH

Part of a block of terraced houses at 89 Upper Warwick Street. Closing as a BH at the turn of the 20th century, the premises were listed as a fried fish dealer in 1908 and a shopkeeper by the 1920's. The pub appears to have been licensed once again and was listed as WSD from the 1930's to the early 1950's. Photographed in the 1890's when the licensee was

Emily J. Hunter.

The continuation of St. James Place southerly is Park Place, then Park Road which together with St. James Street and Park Lane were all once part of the ancient road to Toxteth Park from the town centre. From the 1860's, the vicinity of Park Road became built-up with the familiar terraced streets that rapidly covered the rural area. Pubs were still abundant, although reduced in numbers in the side streets compared to the older parts of the town. The main thoroughfare of Dingle is Park Road which once housed some 40 pubs including the following:

Peacock Inn

Probably the earliest inn of three that were all close to the summit of Park Road. This sketch dates from 1820 when it would have been part of a small hamlet in the countryside to the east of the road. Situated a little south of the present High Park PH near High Park Street, High Park was the highest point of

Toxteth Park and the Peacock Inn was probably a former lodge of the park, apparently built c1635. The premises were also known as the High Park Coffee House but had been demolished by the 1870's as was the High Park Tavern, situated faciing the Peacock, between what would become Wellington Road and Greil Street, both cleared to make way for the ever increasing spread of terraced streets. The Brookfield family family ran the Peacock from the 1820's to the 1870's.

Royal George

The Royal George is open to date, the photograph displays the pub's nickname - 'Blacks' (Black George's)

The Coach & Horses

A former Threlfall's house on the block between Aberdeen Street and South Street. Photographed in the late 1950's when managed by Thomas Melling,

landscaping now covers the site. Listed 1970.
1892 Licensee: James Joseph Webster. Registered Owner: Threlfall's Brewery.

Dingle Hotel

Listed and still trading at 345-347 Park Road at its junction with the former Leonora Street and photographed in 1908 when the licensee was Jessie Appleton (manager 1890's-1920's). The exterior has altered very little over the years. The adjoining shop

was Hughes' pharmacy. After closure for renovation in 1995, the premises reopened as 'Jessie Appleton's'.

Sefton Arms

On the west side of Park Road at its junction with Laxey Street (and locally known as the 'Laxey'). Listed as SV pre-1880's, it was named after the block which clearly states "Sefton Terrace". This view is

from 1908 when the licensee was Edward Wild. Adjoining the pub was a tobacconist run by Miss Catherine Dodd with Alexandra Stamper's hairdressers next to her. Listed 1970.
1892 Licensee: Frederick Pearson. Registered Owner: Smith & Mumford, Brewers.

Crown Vaults

The Crown Vaults at 120 Park Road is currently closed. The photograph is from 1908 when the licensee was Thomas Burke. Cinemas, like the old pubs hold fond memories and the year of the photograph was the start of the boom years for the

cinema. Amongst the adverts on the pub are two for the Tivoli and Park Palace, both cinemas having opened simultaneously on 21 December 1908. The Park Palace, Mill Street had earlier been a theatre whilst the Tivoli, Lime Street had been a place of entertainment since 1847.

1892 Licensee: James Walker Registered Owner: Threlfall's Brewery

Pineapple

The photograph is of the original inn, which was the first structure built west of Park Road. The inn, which was listed in the 1820's, stood in rural surroundings set back off Park Road in a square close to the site of the present David Street, with gardens including a strawberry garden and bowling green extending to what is now the Park Hill Road vicinity. As the ever-engulfing tide of building in the Park Road vicinity crept southerly, this old inn was swept away to make way for more terraced streets. The streets of this vicinity were named after Biblical characters, hence the area's nickname the 'Holy Land'. One of the streets is named Moses Street, on the corner of which the new Pineapple was built. The licensee from the

1850's was Charles Turner, probably the Member of Parliament for South Lancashire whose widow built the nearby Turner Memorial Home for Incurables.

The Swan

A former Higson's house on the corner of Park Road and Drysdale Street. The premises have since been replaced by a large supermarket. The photograph was taken c1964 when the manager was Bernard McGillan. The adjoining shop was George Simmons' paint and wallpaper shop.

MAID OF ERIN

THE SWAN

Mill Street, west of Park Road was laid out c1803 and was then named Bedford Street as far as Warwick Street. As the 19th century progressed, Mill Street gradually became built on further south taking its name from a number of windmills that existed in the vicinity. It eventually contained approximately 37 public houses. The first PH was probably 'The Windmill Tavern' which was listed in the 1830's.

Flat Iron (pictured on page 14)

Aptly named, this large pub was listed at 1-3 Mill Street and 32 St. James Place. It was part of a block named Toxteth Buildings and replaced an earlier pub, the Toxteth Inn. Note a once common sight when photographed in the 1920's - a gentlemen's toilet outside the pub. The premises were demolished in the 1970's and the site landscaped.

Maid of Erin (above right)

Listed at 23 Mill Street. The premises were destroyed by enemy bombing in the war. Photographed in the 1920's when the manager was Harold Williams.

Alton Tower Vaults

The Alton Tower Vaults probably suffered a similar fate to the Maid of Erin since it was not listed after the war. The manager was James Dooley when photographed in 1920's. Pre-1890's, it was named the Liver Vaults and, pre-1870, the Teutonic.

Great Eastern

The Great Eastern is still trading on the corner of Mill Street and Harlow Street (the premises were also

also took the same name: in Cockspur Street (L3), Langsdale Street (L3) and Scotland Road (L5). A former mast of the ship became a flagpole at the Kop end of Liverpool Football Club's ground.

Police report (1903): 'The manager was charged with having a reservist's life certificate in his possession fined 5/-d and costs. Notice of objection.'

Beresford Hotel (below)

Situated on the corner of Mill Street and Beresford Road, it was demolished to create space for houses built during the 1960's and 1970's. Photographed in the 1920's when the manager was Edward Farquhar with Crowton's dairy adjoining.
1892 Licensee: Edward H. Smith. Registered Owner: Thomas May Smith, Brewer

The Grapes (facing top left)

A large pub boasting the distinct blue-tiled frontage common to many Threlfalls pubs, the Grapes stood on the corner of Mill Street and Upper Harrington Street. Photographed in the 1960's when the manager was Alfred George Cook, the premises were demolished in the 1980's.

listed as Liverpool Workingman's Conservative Association from the 1930's to the 1950's). The exterior is little changed from this photograph taken in 1912 when the manager was Stephen Robertson. The premises were first listed as BH in the 1850's. The name Great Eastern first appears in the 1860's, named after the Great Eastern Steam Ship, the biggest ship in the world when launched in 1858. Although the ship was of a revolutionary design, having many new features, she was a failure, largely through financial mismanagement Three other Liverpool pubs

BERESFORD HOTEL

THE GRAPES

Warwick Castle

At 134 Mill Street close to Warwick Street, this 1900 photograph of the Warwick Castle displays the name Marshalls on the window, referring to William James Marshall - manager. Pre-1880's, it was named Mill Vaults. The adjoining shops were Pegrams, belonging to a well-known Liverpool tea merchants and Joseph Griffith's chandlers. Known locally prior to demolition as the 'Rat'. Listed 1964.

1901 Police Report: 'Selling drink to a two drunken men 20/-d and costs each case. Selling drink to a drunken woman £5 and costs. Notice of objection.'

Mosley Arms

Still trading at the junction of Mill Street and the former Mosley Street. The houses of Mosley Street had been demolished, leaving the pub in isolation in

this 1960's view when the licensee was Margaretta Campbell. Named the Windmill Tavern from1860's-1880's, thereafter listed as WSV. The name Mosley Arms appears on a 1940 list.

Two Lions

The Two Lions stood at 190 Mill Street on the corner of Northumberland Street. Note the landing

houses in Northumberland Street in this 1920's photograph. The manager at the time was Mrs. Florence Aitchison, the adjoining shop was Evans and Clement's grocers and is part of the same building as the pub. The pub and landing houses were demolished in the 1970's.

Mersey Forge

Photographed in the early 1960's, the Mersey Forge stood at 346 Mill Street and 42 Harlow Street. The adjoining shops were Lawson's newsagency, Jane's, general dealers and Bob's greengrocery. This pub was named after a large iron works known as the Mersey Forge which was established as early as 1810 and was located either side of nearby Grafton Street, Amongst the work turned out at the Forge was a gun measuring 13 feet long, constructed in 1845 for the American frigate "Princetown". In 1856 the Horsfall Gun, the world's largest gun at that time weighing 21 ton 17 cwt, was built there. In the same year, the gun was tested on the north shore near Formby, firing a 300 lb ball up to five miles. In its heyday, over 1500 men were employed at the works until a gradual decline set in around 1880, culminating in closure in the early years of the l900's. One reminder of the Mersey Forge is Horsfall Street, which once ran right through the works.

Wellington Vaults

Open to date at the junction of Mill Street and Wellington Road and photographed in the 1920's

when the licensee was Thomas Jillings. Clearly displayed is 'Foreign Wine and Spirit Vaults and Wellington Spirit Vaults'. Next door to the pub on Mill Street was Charles Ryan's hairdresser shop, with the adjoining shop on Wellington Road listed as Charles Thomson's pork butcher's shop. The pub is locally known as 'Charlie Fays' or 'Coles'. Pre-1860's, it was listed at 2 Wellington Place (Mill Street terminated here at that time, taking over Wellington

Place when the street was built on further south).

Parallel to Mill Street and closer to the Dock Road stands Grafton Street. Named after the Duke of Grafton, Prime Minister (1766-1770) the street once contained some 20 courts and 21 pubs amongst early terraced property.

WSV (above)

A motley crew stand outside the pub which stood on the corner of Grafton Street and a former court-ridden street, Fisher Street. Photographed in 1900, the premises were sold by Walkers soon after. The former Fisher Street still remains, although there is no trace of any courts. All that remains is a passageway separating modern warehouses.

1892 police report: 'Harbouring police constables whilst on duty. Pending. And selling drink to a drunken man. 20/-d and costs. Notice of objection.'

The Star

The Star, at 195 Grafton Street, faced the Southern Hospital. The street behind was named Star Street and, in the nearby Warwick Street, a pub of the same name still stands. Photographed in the 1890's when the licensee was Mrs. Sarah Ann Pritty. Not listed 1920's. Pre-1860's named the Briton.
1892 Licensee: David John Barr Registered Owner: Cheshire Lines Co. Committee

Mersey View

The Mersey View is the only pub left on the street, standing on the corner of Grafton Street and Park Street, Recently renamed after its nickname - Dirty Dicks, it was earlier named the Mersey Vaults. This photograph is from the 1920's when managed by John Edward Nolan and shows housing long since demolished on either side of the pub, which currently stands in isolation and is closed at the time of writing.

Grafton Street (below)

This 1950's view of Grafton Street shows court property shortly before demolition The majority of courts were located north of the large Mersey Forge works, between Park Street and Parliament Street. A few existed at the south end of the street including these located between Harlow Street and Wellington Road.

Beaufort Street (formerly Bedford Street) once contained 15 pubs and ran parallel with Grafton Street. Since the 1960's, it has been physically broken up with recently built houses in the vicinity.

GRAFTON STREET

Beaufort Arms

The Beaufort Arms stood on the corner of Beaufort Street and Northumberland Street. Before 1914, it was named Northumberland House. Photographed in

the 1950's when the manager was Michael Gilmartin, whose surname was referred to as a nickname and is displayed over the door. This pub had entrances in three streets - two in Beaufort Street, two in Northumberland Street and one in Robertson Street. The photograph is taken from Northumberland Street with Robertson Street on the left and Beaufort Street on the right. The other pub in this view was the Britannia Vaults. Listed 1970.

Beaufort Vaults

Standing on the corner of Beaufort Street and Rutter Street and displaying its nickname Mac's, over

the door in this 1960's photograph when the licensee was Margaret Simpson. Pre-1890's it was named the Grapes. Listed 1970.

Northumberland Street lead in an eastward direction from the Dock Road. Six courts and 20 pubs once existed here amongst the terraced property.

Grapes

Listed at 2 Northumberland Street at the junction with Upper Mann Street, pre-1860's it was called

Bella Vista (fine view). This 1950's photograph shows landing houses which had replaced the slum property of Northumberland Street in the 1930's. Listed 1970. *1892 Licensee: Alice Armistead. Registered Owner: R. Barker & Co., Brewers.*

Britannia Vaults

Listed at 21a Northumberland Street and 225 Beaufort Street, the photograph is from the 1920's when managed by Richard Walsh. 1892 Police Report: 'Permitting drunkenness. Bound over'. Listed 1970.

In common with all the older parts of Liverpool, it will be noticed that numerous pubs closed down between 1900 and 1914. This was mainly due to the Government of the time encouraging magistrates not to issue licences in districts that had too many public houses as a way of reducing the plague of drunkenness that was rampant throughout the country. An interesting insight into running a pub in those days is reported in 1905. Thomas Vernon Burnett heard that the owners of The Grapes, 33 Northumberland Street at the junction with Wolfe Street were looking for a new landlord to run it for them, the previous licensee having lost his license after a police investigation into his conduct on the premises.

Having a military background and being somewhat a disciplinarian, he was considered suitable. Despite the licensing authority warning him that the premises had a bad reputation, he acquired the pub in June 1905.

The squalor, vice and poverty of the area soon become apparent to the new licensee. Trying to keep out prostitutes, thieves and such undesirables and yet keep the customers coming in was a formidable task to someone new to the trade. His wife Madge detested seeing young women donned in their shawls and children tugging at their skirts entering the pub early in the day. Spending money they received from trading their meagre goods at the local pawnbrokers, they

stayed in the pub all day drinking whilst their children went hungry. Hate it or not, it was such people that kept licensees and their families in work. Men too, would often stay all day having called in for a quick pint before going to work, ending up by the fireside rather than the dockside. Sadly, this was the norm for thousands of families living in the squalor that existed along the line of docks in both north and south Liverpool.

Having brought the place an air of respectability, after a year the Burnetts had had enough. The long hours and demands of the job had worn them out. Their young daughter's health was suffering and, in June 1906, they handed the pub over to John Joseph Tyrer, before emigrating to Australia. The pub was to change hands once more before being finally closed by the authorities in 1910.

Further south from Northumberland Street is Park Street which also runs in an easterly direction from the Dock Road to Park Road. Many years ago it was part of a crowded squalid area and, in common with all such areas, pubs were plentiful, with 19 once listed on the street.

Mersey Beat

Listed at 56 Park Street and photographed in the early 1970's when the licensee was Jessie Walsh. Topically named when it was opened in 1967, it

displayed guitars reminiscent of the Mersey Beat era. Although built less than thirty years ago, it has been demolished, apparently due to the premises having serious structural faults and subsidence.

Albion Vaults

Standing at the corner of Park Street and Mill Street and photographed in the 1950's when the licensee was

Mrs Lilly Lowles. Advertising for Star cigarettes can be seen on Arthur Lane's adjoining newsagent. Listed 1964.

Alexandra

Hughson Street runs between Park Street and

Northumberland Street and now contains new houses. This pre-1914 view, when the manager was John Hoyle, shows the pub with its castle-like facade.

Toxteth

Still trading at 141 Park Street at its junction with Park Road and photographed in 1912 when the

licensee was Thomas Mellor, the window advertises 'Mellors and Billiards'. The name on the adjoining shop window was 'W. Leyland and the London'. Although I cannot trace the reason for "London", the shop was a hairdresser's listed to William James Leyland and it advertises 'Haircut 6d'.

1892 Licensee: Isaac Cliffe. Registered Owner: Harding & Parrington, Brewers.

Leaving this immediate location and travelling a little further south is Wellington Road, named after the Duke of Wellington, which once contained 13 pubs.

Herculaneum Bridge Hotel

Listed at 28-30 Wellington Road and named after the nearby dock. No longer a main thoroughfare, Wellington Road once led from Park Road through to Grafton Street. The section where the pub stands is now named Herculaneum Road. Known locally as 'Peg Legs', the photograph is from the 1960's when the manager was John Henry Johnston.

Police Report 1898: 'Back door opens into

enclosed stableyard which is sublet to three persons and the back door of a private house also opens into said yard. When the gate is closed the police have no access to the back of the licensed premises'.

Prince of Wales Hotel

A former Greenall's house standing on the corner of Wellington Road and Bessemer Street when photographed in the early 1960's. A modern pub now occupies this site.

Alabama

A typical corner local located at the junction of Anglesea Street and Tavistock Street (off Wellington Road).

PRINCE OF WALES HOTEL

ALABAMA

Photographed in the 1920's when the manager was George Irwin. The pub was probably named after the ship 'Alabama', built at Laird's, Birkenhead. Leaving Liverpool in 1862 as the "290", it was commissioned into the Confederate Navy and became the scourge of the high seas, destroying over 50 United States vessels from 1862 to 1864. She was finally sunk off Cherbourg, France in June 1864. Listed 1970.

Anglesea (left)

Photographed in the 1950's when the manager was Thomas Charles Lowles, the Anglesea is a small local at the junction of Beresford Road and Anglesea Street.

Rankin Street

The further south that houses were built, the more they became the familiar terraced style still abundant today. Pockets of court property, however, were still built and one such group was in Rankin Street, which contained five courts. Landing houses which replaced the old slum property of this street were themselves demolished in the early 1990's. The Nelson pub can be seen at the bottom of the street in this 1920's view.

Nelson

At the junction of Thornton Place and Rankin Street (originally Holland Street), this huge pub was built more in line with city centre pubs. Named the Rankin when photographed in 1908. Listed as the Nelson from c1912 until demolition in the 1970's.

POETS CORNER

Further south again and another of the many thoroughfares that lead eastward up to Park Road is Park Hill Road, which contained 5 pubs.

Poets Corner (above)

Still trading at the junction of Park Hill Road and Bowring Street, which now contains 1960's housing. Photographed in the 1920's when the manager was Thomas Edward Mason, the pub was also named the Bowring at various dates. The main difference to the building today is that the corner door is no longer in use.

Parkhill Hotel

The Parkhill stood at the junction of Park Hill Road and Beloe Street (originally Bright

Street). Photographed in the 1920's when the manager was James Tamsick Gee. Housing now covers the site. Listed 1970.

Mount

Still trading at the junction of South Hill Road and Dingle Mount, the railings fronting the pub have been

Criterion

A Charrington's house in this 1960's photograph when the licensee was John Carlton. At the junction of South Street and Hawkstone Street, it appears to

removed as have the surrounding buildings. The building to the left was a small cul-de-sac named Dingle Terrace and now a school entrance. The pub is known by its nickname the 'Sixy', from when the pub had a six day licence. The six day licence was a common practice in the late 19th century. At that time, a licence for a pub cost anything from about £4 up to about £60, depending on the rent of the premises. Any victuallers who closed on a Sunday were entitled to one-seventh off the cost of the licence; similarly Victuallers who closed one hour before the time required by law on week days, paid only five-sevenths of their licence. Pre-1914 the pub was named the Baron.

Park Castle Hotel (above right)

A pre-1914 family snap when the manager was William Bateman. Named the Grapes before 1890 and listed at Hawkstone Street (originally Carlisle Street) at its junction with Byles Street. The pub was not listed by the 1940's and was possibly destroyed during the war, its site having long since been replaced by housing. Both streets remain, although Hawkstone Street is not on its original line.

have been extended onto the terraced property some time in the past. A section of South Street, north of Admiral Street, remains. The area where the Criterion stood, south of Admiral Street, was cleared of its old houses and pubs in the 1970's.

Willaloo

The section of South Street mentioned in the previous view as still remaining, was not even built at the time of this 1850's drawing of a small colony of cottages that was known as Willaloo at the north end

of South Street. A tan yard existed at the time (on the site of the present Wynnstay, Veolas, Rhiwlas and Powis Streets) and every Sunday the three BH's were packed with customers, particularly ship-carpenters and workers from the tan yard and the Mersey Forge. Two or three fights took place before dinner time every Sunday. Becoming somewhat of a tradition during the 1830's, there were even look-outs for the police. At that time, there were only two constables in Toxteth and the Bridewell was quite a distance away in Cotter Street. Two constables seem incredible today but, in the early 19th century, the police force was in its infancy. The premises were known by the licensee's surnames: Chadwick's, Brookfield's and Lee's. The first two closed before 1880 while Lee's survived until the 1920's.

Scotia

The Scotia which was listed as a BH pre-1880's stood at the junction of Brenton Street and Digby Street (both abolished) and was in the midst of a maze of terraced streets east of Park Road that were demolished in the 1960's and 70's with the site now covered by what is now Top Rank's new bingo hall. A licence was refused for the pub in 1912 and the

premises were listed as a shop in 1930's. Photographed in 1908 when the manager was James Matthews.

Digby House

A typical local, on the corner of Digby Street and Collins Street (abolished), it was photographed c1960

when the licensee was Margaret Jones. The pub together with the streets was demolished in the 1970's.

Police Report 1892: 'Card and domino playing allowed in this house.'

Digby Arms

Another typical local which stood on the corner of Moville Street (abolished) and Digby Street. Photograph c1960 when the licensee was Mrs. Mary Roberts.

1892 Licensee: Thirza Morrey. Proprietor & Registered Owner: Thirza Morrey.

Castle Inn

Named the Liver before 1890, the Castle stood on the corner of Miles Street and Clevedon Street. Photographed c1960 when managed by John Tooley.

Napier

The Napier, on the corner of Windsor Street and Upper Hill Street closed and was demolished during the 1980's. Photographed in the 1920's when the

manager was George McPherson Dunning, pre-1880's it was listed as Commodore Napier after Lord Napier (1810-1890) famed soldier of the Indian Mutiny (1857/58).

British Standard

Listed at 39-41 Grey Street at the junction with Emerson Street (off Windsor Street) and

NAPIER

RODNEY ARMS

photographed in 1903 when the manageress was Mrs. Mary Greatrex. Over the door is written Fraser, probably an earlier proprietor. Not listed 1950's, new housing now occupies the site.

Rodney Arms

Located at the junction of Admiral Street and Chipping Street and photographed in 1912, when the manager was James Dunn. The site of Chipping Street is now grassland adjoining Admiral Street police station. Listed 1970.

Old Stingo

A Mellor's house at the junction of High Park Street and Greta Street (abolished on its original line) Photograph c1960 when managed by Arthur Phillips. Pre-1914, it was named the Toxteth Park Hotel. Landscaping replaces this pub. Listed 1970.

Victoria

Whittaker Street (originally Calvin Street - abolished) was a thoroughfare off Windsor Street which led through to Berkley Street at whose junction this former pub was located. Photographed c1960 when the manager was George Alcock, the site is now part of a sports ground.

Empress Hotel

Still trading on the corner of High Park Street and Wellington Terrace, there has been little change to the exterior of this building from this 1920's photograph when managed by John Talbot. The main difference is the signage: Wines and Spirits have replaced Empress, with Traditional Ales replacing Hotel, whilst in the centre is now written: 'This building appears on the album sleeve of Ringo Starr's first solo album 'Sentimental Journey'. (Ringo Starr, drummer with The Beatles, was born close to this pub)

Upper Parliament Street was the home of the more wealthy merchants of the town during the last century and early 20th century, yet slum property did exist especially at the summit of the street where it met Smithdown Lane and Falkner Street. The area was cleared in the 1930's.

Beehive

This old PH was listed at the corner of Holden Street (abolished) and Pine Grove. Henry Jones was manager during the 1890's when this photograph was taken of a delivery of beer in progress. The pub closed in the 1920's.
1892 Licensee: William Worthington Registered Owner: Cook Bros, Brewers

Falkner Street, although north of Upper Parliament Street (which is Liverpool 7) is listed as Liverpool 8 due to the old irregular boundaries. Originally Crabtree Lane, it was renamed after Edward Falkner who enrolled some 1000 men in defence of Liverpool when a French invasion was imminent in 1797. The street has been physically split, with listed buildings still abundant in the section leading eastward from Hope Street at the edge of the city centre. Demolition occurred further east during the 1960's & 1970's and near its summit at Smithdown Lane. Some 17 pubs once stood here.

Falkner

At the junction of Falkner Street and Bloom Street and photographed c1960 when managed by Leslie

Cheetham. In the thirty years since this photograph, modern housing has been built and demolished, a common feature throughout the inner areas. Pre-1880's, the pub was named Bloom Vaults.
1892 Licensee: Thomas Downey. Registered Owner Cook Bros., Brewers.

Brown Cow

Photographed in 1903 where it appears the licensee (listed as Mary Kelly) and her family are posing for the photographer. The Brown Cow was at the junction of Harding Street and Milner Street. The old property seems to have been a warehouse. On the wall is written Milner Street - late Barton Street. This street was only 22 yards long in a slum-ridden area that was cleared during the 1930's.

Crown Vaults

A small local pub (recently demolished) on the corner of Falkner Street and Holden Street whose houses were pulled down in the 1970's. The photograph is from c1960 when the licensee was Vincent Anthony Carroll.

Police Report (1901): 'Quoits played. Also selling drink to a drunken man. Dismissed.'

Falkner Arms

Named the Royal Standard before 1880, the Falkner Arms was listed at 282 Falkner Street. A court

entrance can be clearly seen adjoining the premises in this pre-1914 photograph when the manager was John Burton. Listed to fried fish dealer in the 1920's

The lower end of Falkner Street is now part of a conservation area where many Georgian and early Victorian dwellings avoided the bulldozer that cleared so many other parts of Liverpool. One such street is St. Bride Street (off Falkner Street), a narrow street now mainly converted into flats. Number 24 at the junction with Little Bride Street is one such flat but was once a beer house having an entrance in both St Bride Street and Little Bride Street. An 1892 Police Report regarding this Bent's Brewery beer house stated: 'Licensee was cautioned by the justices at the last annual sessions as to allowing card playing. It is still carried on but not so frequently as formerly.'

Lowther Castle

A former Ind Coope house on the corner of Lowther Street and Almond Street. Photographed in the late 1960's when managed by George Eaton. Like

others in the area, the houses of Lowther Street and Almond Street have been demolished after little more than twenty years construction.

Pavilion

On the other side of Upper Parliament Street stands Lorton Street where this pub was located at its junction with Buttermere Street. Named after a

former theatre on Lodge Lane which is now a bingo hall, the pub closed and was demolished during the 1980's. Photographed in 1908 when managed by Frederick Coop. Pre-1880's it was named The Grapes.

Sixteen pubs were listed on Lodge Lane which runs south from the top of Upper Parliament Street to Sefton Park Road. The name derives from a former lodge of Toxteth Park.

DART

Dart (opposite)

Still trading on the corner of Lodge Lane and Longfellow Street. This view is from the 1920's when managed by Charles Maguire. Known locally as 'Spaggs', the Dart is currently standing in isolation.

WSV (right)

On the corner of Lodge Lane and Cedar Grove, the pub was photographed in the 1920's when the manager was William Smith Seller. The pub was demolished in the 1970's and its site has been landscaped.

The Boundary

A substantial pub on the corner of Lodge Lane and Smithdown Road, the Boundary reopened in 1994 after a period of closure. The present structure displays a date of 1902 although a pub was listed here earlier. From the 1860's to 1880's, it was listed as the Clarendon and then a BH until the premises were rebuilt in 1902. This view is from the 1920's when managed by Thomas Burns.

BH

A typical terraced house on the corner of Cedar Grove and Maple Grove which, pre-1914, was one of

the many BHs around the city. When photographed, the licensee was Mrs. Mary Jane Elliott. The licence for this particular BH expired in 1917. The building was listed as a shop in the 1930's. The property still stands as a dwelling house.

BH

Photographed in 1908 when managed by John Alfred Cann, this old BH on Maple Grove at its corner

with Lime Grove closed c1919. The building reopened as a beer retailer during the 1930's until the 1950's. The premises were demolished c1970 and the site is now open land.

Windsor Hotel

Beaumont Street (formerly Stanhope Street) is to the west of Lodge Lane. The Windsor Hotel is on the corner of Beaumont Street and Kingsley Road and this

WINDSOR HOTEL

splendid view shows the pub in the 1920's when the lamps on the surrounding railings would have made a wonderful sight at night. The manager at the time was Henry Frederick Shaw. The railings, lamps, and surrounding houses have all now been demolished. The pub, which is closed at the time of writing, still displays a clock over the door from which it gained its nickname 'The Clock'.

Stanhope Street, renamed Beaumont Street in the 1860's, was one of only a couple of streets built south of Upper Parliament Street at its upper end in the 1840's, when the area was called Windsor. The first structure on the street's south side was a church, St. Clements, indicating a parish soon to be built. The church opened in 1841 (at that time a rope-walk existed immediately behind the church) and, rather

surprisingly, has survived to the present day. When the church opened, the vicinity was still open land. Within twenty years after the construction of St. Clements, the area south of the church was covered by a maze of terraced streets, the majority having since been demolished although, a little further afield, many still remain around Lodge Lane, Kingsley Road, and Granby Street.

Cambridge Hotel

A Bent's house at the corner of Alt Street (which led from Beaumont Street to Tiber Street) and Cam Street. One of formerly 7 pubs listed in Alt Street. Photographed in the 1960's, when managed by Elsie Mary Owens and known locally as the Cam, modern houses now stand on the site.
1892 Licensee: Emily Metcalf. Proprietor: Bent's Brewery Co.

Parliament

Standing at the corner of Alt Street and Thames Street. Photographed during the 1960's when managed by John Benjamin Dent. In common with many other streets, housing built only a couple of decades ago has been cleared with recently built housing now occupying the area. Listed 1964.

Gladstone Hotel

Listed No. 32-34 Dove Street (originally Church Street and presumably named after the Church of St Clements, the side of which was in the street) led through to Solway Street pre-1980's. Pre-1914, the pub, one of three in the street, was named the Turtle Dove. Photographed c1960 when managed by Edward Parr, modern housing now fills the site.

Solway Arms

   Photographed in the 1920's when the manager was Thomas Foster, the Solway was at the junction of Alt Street and Solway Street. Modern housing now occupies the site. Listed 1970.
1892 Licensee: William Harrison. Registered Owner: R. Barker & Co., Brewers, Huyton.

Leaving the Liverpool 8 district, we now enter Edge Hill (Liverpool 7) and commence with a main thoroughfare - Prescot Street, which once had 9 pubs.

Three Tuns

Pre-1890's listed as BH & brewer at the junction of Prescot Street with Fortescue Street (originally Sherwood Street - abolished). The name of this pub is of ancient date, like the more commonly named Grapes indicating that beer and wine were sold on the premises in the days when most people could neither read or write. Photographed in the 1920's when managed by Joseph Crossley, the premises closed in the 1960's. The pub and former street are now part of the surrounds of the Royal Liverpool Hospital.

Prior to the 1980's, Crown Street led from the top of Pembroke Place in a southerly direction to Upper Parliament Street. The street has since been physically broken up with a section remaining from Pembroke Place to just beyond Paddington. Continuing southerly, the building of the Police Traffic Control Headquarters has replaced part of the street and surrounding area; beyond here a section of the street still remains. Nearing Upper Parliament Street, housing built some twenty years ago known as the St Nathaniel's estate has recently been cleared, with part of the site accommodating a new hospital. There were 18 pubs on Crown Street.

Royal William

The only pub left on Crown Street and currently closed. Named after the first Liverpool steam ship to cross the Atlantic from Liverpool in 1838, the

outward passage taking 19 days. A picture of the ship is currently displayed, painted over the advert for "Double Diamond" on this 1960's view. The modern buildings in the background are part of the University.

Palace Inn

At the junction of Crown Street and Blanche Street which was only 70 yards long (abolished). Pre-1880's, the pub was named The Havelock. Photographed c1960 when managed by Veronica Conway. The pub

was demolished in the 1970's and the site is now part of the police traffic headquarters.

Market Inn

At the corner of Crown Street and Grant Street which was only 50 yards long (abolished) and led into Vine Street. The pub closed c1940 and the premises were listed in the 1950's as a private house. The site is now a grassed area. Photographed c1904 when the

pub was managed by Mrs Jane Scott, probably the woman in the doorway.

Railway Inn

So named because it was close to the old railway terminus that stood here as a passenger terminal before Lime Street Station opened. The photograph was taken in 1904 when managed by George Thatcher. Not listed 1912.

Police Report 1892: 'Wife of licensee holds the license of beer house, 14 Silvester Street.'

Huskisson Vaults

Named after William Huskisson MP, who was the first person to be killed by a train, at the opening ceremony of the world's first major passenger railway between Liverpool and Manchester on September 15th. 1830. The Huskisson Vaults stood at the corner of Crown Street and Pine Grove (with the old

Boundary Vaults

The Boundary Vaults stood at the corner of Falkner Street and Crown Street, on the boundary of Liverpool 7 and 8. Photographed in the 1890's, the name displayed over the window read 'Gent Wine & Spirit Merchants' on Crown Street and 'Gents Wine & Spirit Stores' on Falkner Street. Amongst the onlookers is a policeman standing by an early type of gas lamp. In 1889 Martha Gent is listed as licensee whilst in 1891/1898 it was Samuel Gent. The adjoining premises, partially shown in the photograph were listed to Arnold Richardson, veterinary surgeon and shoeing & forge yard, whose name is partially shown. The shop on Falkner Street was a milk dealer in 1908, later cocoa rooms. The pub closed during the 1950's.

1892 Licensee: Samuel Gent. Registered Owner: Rev. Henry Finch

irregular boundaries, Pine Grove was in Liverpool 8). Photograph c1968 when the licensee was Jean Linton. The adjoining shop was Alma's Hairdresser and the church in Pine Grove (recently demolished) was St Nathaniels (1868).

Oxford

Photographed c1960 when the licensee was Ethel Franco and open to date at the junction of Oxford Street and Florist Street (abolished) and now, since the

Myrtle Street which is the continuation of Hardman Street eastward from the city centre, once contained 14 pubs. A modern pub, the Carousel, is the only one still trading.

reconstruction of the vicinity, the only old structure left on this section of the street. The adjoining shop was formerly listed to Nicholas W. Stephen Ltd., tobacco merchants and cigar importers, and has been replaced by landscaping.

Salisbury (top right)

An Ind Coope house, on the corner of Oxford Street and Bamber Street which was demolished in the 1970's. The former Bamber Street, is now incorporated into the site of the Police Traffic HQ. Photograph from approximately 1960 when managed by Frederick O'Brien

Red House (right)

The pub stood on the corner of Crown Street and Oxford Street. Photographed c1970, the site is now landscaped.
1892 Licensee: John Dunbar. Registered Owner: Harding & Parrington Brewers.

Myrtle

At the junction of Myrtle Street and Mulberry Street, this photograph from the 1920's shows an ice-

cream man surrounded by children. The actual site of the pub is now a landscaped part of the University precinct. Listed 1970.

Palatine Hotel

The pub stood at the corner of Myrtle Street and junction of Heath Street (abolished). Photographed c1964 when when the manager was Patrick Mooney. The adjoining shop was Killip & Sons' fishmongers. The site is now part of Myrtle Parade Shopping Arcade.

1892 Licensee: Alex. McKinnell Registered Owner: John Bramley, Brewer, Upper Hill Street

Mona

A former Higson's pub at the junction of Myrtle Street and Mona Street (abolished). Pre-1880's named the Grapes Inn. A child sits on the step in this 1960's photograph when managed by Terence Joseph McConnon. The premises were demolished in the 1970's.

Police Report 1892: 'The Licensee is employed as a barman at 121 Walton Breck Road and appears to take no part in the management of the business.' (The pub mentioned is the Salisbury Hotel, open to date).
1892 Licensee: Jesse Thwaites. Registered Owner: Thomas & J. Bernard, Brewers, Edinburgh.

The Mulberry Bush

The Mulberry Bush stood on Mulberry Street, which crosses over Myrtle Street northward from Catharine Street, then across Oxford Street into the grounds of the University. The section where this pub stood at its junction with Chesnut Street is now part of the University's grounds. The premises were demolished c1960. Photographed in the 1920's when the manager was Isaiah Hallaway. Pre-1914 the pub was named the Grapes.

Close to this pub stood the Chestnut Arms which during the 1950's was frequented by a friend of mine, Ted Williams, who recalls: 'it was referred to as "Mrs Mac's and amongst its customers were students and staff from the university. The pub had a tremendous atmosphere. The ceiling had many names inscribed on it, some famous and others mainly ex-university residents. The only fault with the pub was it only had one toilet, so if you took a wife or girlfriend there for the night and she had to use the WC, you would have to stand guard!' After its demolition many of the patrons then drank in the nearby Mulberry Bush but this too was demolished in the early 1960s. A modern pub, the Augustus John now stands in the vicinity.

Portland Arms

Pre-1914 named the Liver Vaults and standing on the corner of Myrtle Street and Melville Place. The photograph taken in the 1890's, when the manager was David Charles Evans, shows a delivery in progress from a horse and cart. The adjoining shop belonged to Charles Williams - a tallow chandlers. (Maker/seller of tallow candles, which were made up from animal fats, especially from sheep and oxen). The site was cleared in the 1970's and new housing for students has recently been built on the site.

Another main thoroughfare in the area that still remains is Smithdown Lane, one of the town's oldest highways. Derived from Esmedurle, an ancient manor mentioned in the Domesday Book whose exact location is now lost in history although thought to have been on the former Great Heath located south of the old pool. Smithdown Lane contained 13 pubs.

STORE VAULTS

Store Vaults

A former Ind Coope house on the corner of Smithdown Lane and Aigburth Street (abolished). Photographed in the mid-1960's when the licensee was Annie Caslin. Pre-1880's, it had a strange name for it's location, the Everton Beacon. The adjoining shops were the Horse Shoe Greeting Card Co and Mrs. Marjorie Williams' newsagency. The premises were demolished during the 1970's.

1892 Licensee: Mary Jane Lloyd. Proprietor: W Jones, Brewer, Edge Vale.

The Matlock (bottom left)

Currently closed and the only pub remaining (at the junction with Oxford Street East). Pre-1880's it was named the Guiding Star. The houses shown to the left on Smithdown Lane surprisingly avoided the mass demolition of the area, of the 1960's and 1970's.

Police Report 1892: 'Quoit and card playing allowed in this house.'

Sefton Hotel

On the corner of Smithdown Lane and Portwood Street (abolished). Close to the top of Upper Parliament Street, the huge Entwistle House looms in

THE MATLOCK

SEFTON HOTEL

the background. Once the largest of the city's multi-storey blocks and built in 1964, it has since been demolished along with the pub. The Store Vaults can be seen at the other junction.

Phoenix

Photographed c1960 when the licensee was Margaret Whitty, the pub stood at the junction with Sophia Street (abolished) and was aptly known as the Flat House.

Four pubs were all named after the large Spekeland Estate which once stood in this vicinity. Spekeland House and its surrounds occupied a large tract of land

north of Smithdown Road and east of Tunnel Road.

Spekeland Arms

Formerly located near the summit of Smithdown Lane at its junction with Chatsworth Street and currently the site of a school playground. Photographed c1970 when George Henry Hughes was

the manager. The adjoining shop was Kennedy Cross & Co., auctioneers. The premises were demolished in the 1970's.

Spekeland Castle

Prior to the 1980's, the east end of Tunnel Road was a maze of terraced streets.
The Spekeland Castle, known locally as the 'Red Brick', stood on the corner of Wrayburn Street and Spekeland Road. Photographed in the 1960's when the

manager was Cyril Bell. A small housing estate now covers this vicinity.
1892 Licensee: Alex. E. Griffiths. Proprietor: William Jones, Brewer, Edge Vale.

The Spekeland

PHOENIX

The Spekeland, the fourth of the "Speke" pubs, is open to date although trading in isolation as the only pub left on Tunnel Road. Known locally as 'Joney's', this view is from the 1920's when the manager was George Tarleton Bibby. The other "Speke" pub was the Spekeland Inn, 42 Albert Road.

BH (bottom)

A typical pre-First World War BH, just a two-up, two-down house that was licensed. The premises, named the Primrose in the 1890s, were located at the junction of Wilfer Street with Spekeland Road. The premises lost its licence in 1908 when the manageress was Miss Alice Bradley, probably the woman in the doorway with her family. The premises were later reopened as a beer retailer until closure in the early 1950s.

BH (next page)

Another typical BH in Wilfer Street, it also lost its licence in 1908. It was later re-established as an ordinary terraced house. Photograph from the 1890's when the manageress was Mrs. Eileen Wheeler.

Earl Marshall Hotel (below)

Still trading in Earle Road, previously between Barnett Street (next to Wilfer Street) and Lindsay Street but now surrounded by modern housing. Earle Road was originally laid out through the Spekeland Estate and named after the Earle family, former owners of the land. This view from the 1920's, when the manager was Thomas Golding, shows the old housing of Lindsay Street with a group of children under the old gas lamp.

The following pubs were all situated east of Smithdown Lane and south of Wavertree Road. The area was a maze of terraced streets until the 1960's and 70's, and is now a large housing estate named the Chatsworth Estate which, in common with many similar estates of Liverpool built only two or three decades ago, is in the process of demolition or renovation.

Chatham Hotel

Many streets as we know them today had their names changed during the last century. Overbury Street was previously Lord Street where there was a

public house named the Queens Arms listed in the 1850's. The street was renamed Overbury Street c1865 and the pub also changed its name to the Black Bottle, which remained until the early 1890's before changing to its current name (the premises were probably rebuilt about this time). Still trading and probably named after William Pitt, first Earl of Chatham and Prime Minister (1756).

Overbury Arms

The pub stood at the corner of Overbury Street and Cardwell Street (originally Clarence Street) which now contains modern housing. Photographed c1968 when managed by Mary Flanagan, the premises were demolished in the 1970's. Next door was a boot repairers listed to John Payne but empty and awaiting demolition in this photograph.

BH

Highgate Street (originally High Street) still remains minus its old property. This old BH photographed in the 1890's was managed by Alice Webster and closed in 1919. The site and vicinity have been replaced by municipal housing. Prior to closure the premises were named the Bricklayer's Arms.

Police Report 1901: 'Unjust measure in use. 10/-d and 7/6d costs.' From 1903: 'Kitchen window of adjoining house looks into yard of this house. There is access from the cellar of this house to the yard and communication could be made without the police being aware of it.' (I wonder if the pub had "stay behinds"?)

Kingslake Street ran parallel to Highgate Street and was originally named King Street which housed a pub aptly named the Kings Arms. Chatsworth Street still runs through the modern estate on its original line although with ongoing improvements to the estate. In 1994 the street was renamed Chatsworth Drive.

Pakington Arms

A former BH on the corner of Chatsworth Street and Pakington Street (abolished).

Photographed c1960 when the licensee was Mrs. Annie Tinker, the premises were demolished in the 1970's.

Craven Heifer

This unusual named pub on the corner of Goulden Street (which was only 74 yards long) and Lovat Street

(both off Chatsworth Street but now demolished) would have been more fitting in Yorkshire where a Craven Heifer is a breed of cow. Photographed in the early 1970's before demolition.
1892 Licensee: Amelia Dacre. Proprietor: Sykes Porter & Co, Brewer, Holly Street.

The Clock

This former Higsons pub photographed c1960 was

on Edgeware Street (abolished) at the junction with Chandos Street (off Chatsworth Street). Listed 1970.
1892 Licensee: W.J. McLoughlin Registered Owner: G. H. Page, Victualler, 55 Harbord Street.

The Neptune

A former Bents house on Harbord Street (taking up the block between Chatsworth Street and Layland Street) So named since the 1950's, prior to this it was the Harbord and pre-1890's, the Napier. Photographed c1960 when managed by Renee Williams.

Tunnel Road is a main thoroughfare in a north/south direction, named after the railway tunnel from Edge Hill to Lime Street. Little of the old property remains.

Railway

At the junction of Tunnel Road and Wavertree Road and facing Edge Hill Station until its demolition in the 1970's. Landscaping now replaces this large pub. The adjoining shop, Doyle's newsagency traded from before the 1st World War until the 1970's.
Police Report 1895: 'Permitting violent conduct. Dismissed. The members of a supposed betting club in the neighbourhood frequent this house.'

Tunnel Hotel (right)

Set back a little off Tunnel Road. A Burtonwood pub managed by Ernest Panther when photographed in the early 1960's. It may well have been a private house early in the last century before its first licensed name of London & North Western Family & Commercial Hotel. The premises were demolished during the 1970's.

1892 Licensee: Ellen Monk. Registered Owner: London & North West Railway Company, 117 Dale Street.

New Pavilion

A typical late-19th century pub where some detail has gone into its construction. Pre-1914 named Tarbuck's Hotel, the pub's nickname was 'Macaulay's due to its location at the junction with Macaulay Street

(abolished) The site is now landscaped. Photographed c1960 when managed by James McNally. Listed 1970. *1892 Licensee: Joseph Voyle. Registered Owner: Tarbuck's Brewery, Richmond Row.*

Paddington

A bustling major road when photographed in the 1930's. The continuation of Brownlow Hill from the city centre eastward, since the mass demolition of the area during the 1960's and 70's, Paddington has all but been obliterated. A tiny section remains with a modern school, Archbishop Blanche, now occupying a large portion of the thoroughfare and surrounding streets.

One pub remains from 14 that once stood on Paddington, with three of the former pubs shown on this view. Centre left is the Greyhound at the junction with Parron Street. The other two facing Parron Street were the Albert and Albert Inn.

Bear's Paw

Open to date and the only pub left on Paddington on the corner of Irvine Street. The photograph was

taken in the 1960's when a Higson's house. So named from the 1850's, except for approximately ten years between the 1870's & 80's when it was named the Royal Duke.

Hall Lane (originally named Mount Vernon) runs north-eastward from Edge Lane to Prescot Street and Kensington and once had six pubs.

The Majestic

Pre-1880's named Volunteer Arms and now the only building with the exception of a church still remaining on the west side of Hall Lane. Photographed when open in the 1980's although the premises are currently closed. Police Report 1892: The husband of the licensee holds the license of the

public house - 63 Belmont Road. The licensee appears to take little part in the management of the house, visiting it only occasionally. The game of parlour quoits allowed.'

Star

Standing alone and derelict while awaiting demolition when photographed in the early 1970's. In the background, the Royal Liverpool Hospital is in the process of construction.

Apollo Vaults

A Birkenhead Brewery house standing on the corner of Hall Lane and Warburton Street when photographed in the 1960's. The adjoining shops were Alexander's dry cleaners and the Pong Lee Laundry. The site is now landscaped.
1892 Licensee: Elizabeth Jellicoe. Registered Owner: Birkenhead Brewery Co.

Alexandra Hotel

The pub stood at the corner of Hall Lane and Bengal Street. The premises were demolished in the 1980's.

Admiral

On the corner of Hall Lane and Tillotson Street. The three storey houses of the steep Tillotson Street were still standing when photographed in the late 1960's. The adjoining shops were all empty awaiting demolition. The site is now landscaped and Tillotson Street is now part of the surrounds of the Royal Liverpool Hospital.

1892 Licensee: William Robinson. Registered Owner: Robert Blezard, Brewer, Scotland Road.

Pembroke Castle

A bare looking pub just showing a small Walker's

sign when photographed in the 1960's. In a list from the 1890's, the pub had four entrances - two in Mount Vernon Street, one in Mount Vernon View and one in Bengal Street. Just shown to the right of the pub are the back of the houses of Bengal Street, an early type of terraced houses which had no upper windows. Mount Vernon refers to Mount Vernon Hall which was located east of Hall Lane.

Mason Street

Mason Street, although named after a timber merchant named Edward Mason c1800, is better known as the home of one of Liverpool's great 19th century eccentrics - Joseph Williamson. After amassing a fortune from the tobacco trade, he began building underground tunnels from the sandstone cellar of his house. Apparently functionless, some were huge caverns, others passages which eventually covered a large area of Edge Hill. It is possible they were even built beyond as they have never been fully explored or mapped and over the years have been filled in or bricked up. One great underground hall under Paddington was some 90 feet high. He also had

houses built in the vicinity which were rented out at very reasonable rates. It seems the reason for these excavations was simply to give employment to scores of labourers and unemployed soldiers returning from the Napoleonic Wars. Creating this work earned him the title of "The Mole" or "King of Edge Hill"; indeed to many families he was a king, saving them from destitution. The cellars of the two pubs at the corner of Mason Street and Grimfield Street were apparently built by Williamson.

It is known that many pubs around Liverpool, particularly the city centre and along the Everton/Edge Hill ridge once contained tunnels. It may well be that Joseph Williamson was responsible for their construction all those years ago.

During September, 1996, a portion of the tunnels was open for two days for the public to view and the interest was phenomenal with over a thousand people coming to view them. Hopefully, those involved in trying to save these unique tunnels will succeed in creating a tourist attraction for future generations and can once again create employment in clearing the tons of rubble to gain access to the "forgotten" network under Edge Hill.

Wavertree Road is a major road through Edge Hill and currently contains 5 pubs, reduced from a former total of 21.

Weighing Machine

Still trading at the junction of Wavertree Road and Marmaduke Street (originally Duke Street). Named the Rose in the 1870's, then listed as a WSV until c1912 when it acquired its current name. The photograph was taken before the First World War when managed by William Nuttall. It now displays

'Established 1863' in place of Warrington Ales Wines & Spirits shown in this view. (A pub of the same name was located not too far from here, in Chatham Street, which closed c1960).

London and North Western

Photographed in the early 1970's, the pub was on the corner of Wavertree Road and Dodge Street

(abolished). Named after Edge Hill Station, which it faced, the premises were originally the North Western Hotel.

Botanic Hotel

Named along with the Botanic House (open to date a little further down Wavertree Road) after Liverpool's Botanic Gardens, adjacent to Botanic Road. The Botanic Hotel stood on the corner with Byford Street (abolished). Photographed c1970, the adjoining shops were Coxell's tobacconist and Bill Taylor's commission agents.

Edge Hill Coffee House

Probably the oldest pub on the road (listed 1820's) and located in the original village area of Edge Hill, it was trading when the vicinity was rural in the early

19th century. Facing the premises is the Church of St. Mary which opened in 1813 and was paid for by Edward Mason (from whom Mason Street gets its name). The pub is closed at the time of writing. Photographed c1970 when the manager was Cyril Roberts and the adjoining shop was Austworth's tobacconist.

Woodside Hotel

A large pub on the corner of Wavertree Road and Woodside Street. Photographed c1960 when managed by Gladys Richards. Note the Ethel Austin shop next door, a company still trading successfully today. Listed 1970.

HOLLAND PLACE,
EDGEHILL, LIVERPOOL

BEARS PAW

Woodside

On the opposite corner of Woodside Street and having the same name, a former Walker's house which was considerably smaller and an older building. Named the Railway Inn pre-1880's. Managed by Ellen Roberts when photographed c1960, the shop next door was the Central Electric Company, television and radio suppliers. Listed 1970.

Grapes Hotel

The Grapes stood on the corner of Wavertree Road and Chatsworth Street. The site is now landscaped, surrounding a modern police station. Pre-1914, the pub was named the Chatsworth. Listed 1970.

The Uxbridge

Named after its street, Uxbridge Street, which still remains as a small "cut" into Wavertree Road, with a police station on one side and landscaping on the

other. Photographed c1960 when managed by James Henry Joseph Dudley.

Leaving this locality, although still in Liverpool 7, the following pubs were/are in various parts of the area, the first two in Smithdown Road.

Mulliner

Smithdown Road has two postal districts, 7 and 15. The Mulliner and Newstead Abbey are in Liverpool 7, on the corner of Mulliner Street. This distinctive

building has recently been refurbished, prior to which it was named the Brook Farm (before the land was built on, a farm named Brook Farm existed here as part of the Spekeland estate).

Newstead Abbey

Still trading at the junction of Smithdown Road and Newstead Street. The pre-1914 photograph shows a

rare sight for the time - plants displayed around the pub; the manager - Joseph Thomas Lester obviously having "green fingers". Known locally as the 'Irish House', the corner door is no longer in use.

Spofforth

Open to date on Spofforth Road, off Picton Road, the last street of Liverpool 7. Beyond here the district becomes Liverpool 15 (which is where the side street in this view, Cadogan Street, is listed). The photograph is from the 1920's when the manager was Albert Holt and there has been little alteration to the exterior over the years. The street and pub were named after one of the greatest Australian cricketers, Frederick Robert Spofforth (1853-1926), nicknamed

the "demon bowler". Born in Balmain, a suburb of Sydney, after leaving Australia, he moved to England, playing for Derbyshire from 1889 until 1891. He died in Long Ditton, Surrey. He made five tours of England between 1878 and 1886 and, in May 1878 at Lords, he humbled the great WC Grace, capturing 6 for 4 and 5 for 16, as the Australians beat the MCC in one day. At the Oval in 1882 (the first Ashes match) he bowled Australia to victory with 14 for 90. The Guinness Book of Records states that in 1881 he clean bowled all 10 wickets in both innings in a match.

Caledonian Hotel

A large pub showing the name Cains high over the door, the Caledonian was on the corner of Holt Road

and Minto Street. Photographed in the 1920's when managed by Oswald Scott, the pub was demolished in the early 1970's and the site is now covered by new housing fronting Minto Close.

Liver Vaults

Open to date on Gilead Street, one of a number of terraced streets west of Holt Road. Photographed in

the early 1960's when an Ind Coope house managed by John Mann. The sign on the gable end, since removed, read Balm Street Passage. The streets Gilead and Balm together with Solomon Street were named after a "quack" - Samuel Solomon who sold a concoction named Balm of Gilead in the late 18th & early 19th centuries. Making a fortune from his "cure", he had a huge mansion built named Gilead House, off Kensington. The three streets were laid out during the 1850's.

Grove Inn

Listed at Botanic Grove which was only 51 yards long (off Clint Street) and photographed in the 1960's

when the manager was Maxwell Peter Ashworth. Clint Street remains, containing new housing between Durning Road and Botanic Road.

Shipperies

Open to date on Durning Road, the continuation of Holt Road southward. This view is from the early 1960's when managed by Stanley Duff. The premises

were named after the Liverpool Shipperies Exhibition of 1886 at the nearby Exhibition Hall. Shown slightly to the left was a former fire station, currently in use as a tyre business.

Half Way House

Located on the corner of Kensington and Gilead Street and open to date as one of only two pubs on the southside of Kensington. Photographed in 1908 when the manager was John Hall. The adjoining shops were John Whitehead's cycle shop and Daniel Higgin's butcher's shop. The shops and remainder of the block have been replaced by landscaping.

The continuation of Kensington is Prescot Road. Numbering of this road varied considerably due to the road once running the length of three different districts: Fairfield (or Stanley), Old Swan and Knotty Ash. It was one of the first turnpike routes of Liverpool in the 18th century originally encompassing London Road, Prescot Street, Kensington, Prescot Road and East Prescot Road.

Edinburgh and Fairfield Arms

Although still in Liverpool 7, these pubs are in the Fairfield district, named after Fairfield Hall, a large mansion which once stood in the area. A rare sight nowadays, with two adjoining pubs still trading. The early view is from the 1890's, when the manager of the Edinburgh was Robert Waddell and the manager of the adjoining Fairfield Arms was Herbert Morris. The second view shows another storey added to the Edinburgh. The Edinburgh was listed at the junction of Nursery Street until 1898, the street then changing to its present name, Laburnum Road.

The following pubs were all in Liverpool 13 with the first five in Prescot Road.

Cattle Market Hotel

Still trading and named after the former (adjacent) cattle market that opened here in 1830 when it was removed from Kirkdale. Photographed c1908 when the licensee was Arthur W. Nelson, the premises were replaced by the present pub in 1931.

Police Report (1902): Serving a man with beer during prohibited hours on a Sunday. Dismissed.

Stanley Hotel

Open to date, the pub opened in the late 1850's as the New Stanley Arms. From 1881 it was named the Stanley Hotel (and possibly re-built). Prior to 1856, an older inn stood on the same site, the White Hart. This name is one of the oldest in the country. In 1393 Richard II made it compulsory for publicans to exhibit a sign. The White Hart was adopted as a badge by him and it became a popular pub sign through out the kingdom. An old sandstone wall still exists outside the premises which might have been part of the old inn, separating the pub from the grounds of St Anne's Church (1831) and old tombstones still remain adjacent to the wall. The former stable is now in use as a garage.

Old Stanley Arms

Still trading facing the Stanley Hotel. Named the Stanley Arms in the 1850's, then from c1860 the Original Stanley Arms Hotel. "Original" was dropped in the 1890's and "Old" adopted. The former stable entrance is shown on this view, and cobblestones still exist to the rear. The pub replaced an earlier inn named the Bull.
1903 Licensee: Joseph Murphy. Registered Owner: Ind Coope & Co.

Old Swan Vaults

This name derives from the first inn of the vicinity the Swan, built in the early 18th century and located at the junction of Prescot Road and Broadgreen Road

(originally Petticoat Lane) The inn's name derived from an ancient family named Walton who owned most of the land hereabouts. Three Swans was the emblem on the family's coat-of-arms. By the 1840's, the name was changed to the Original Old Swan. From this date, the inn was listed as 2 Swan Row, Prescot Road. This remained until c1880 when it was re-addressed as 225 Prescot Road. The old inn was demolished and replaced by the present structure in the 1890's, then named the Old Swan Vaults Two name changes have occurred since the 1980's; the Red House and, currently, First Avenue.

Old Swan Hotel

A former 18th century coaching inn standing at the junction of Broadgreen Road and open to date. Photographed c1912 when the licensee was Joseph Broster.

The adjoining three storey block on St. Oswald Street still remains. The pub which was built c1775 is supposedly the oldest structure in the vicinity. A former block of shops known as Hoults Corner used to stand facing the pub at the junction of St. Oswald

Street and Prescot Road until demolition c1940. The name was taken from James Hoult, a licensee of the Pub in the 1840's. He was a prominent local resident who, besides running the pub, was one of a number of local residents who controlled the old toll bars in and around Old Swan. He also ran the first omnibuses from Liverpool to Knotty Ash.
1903 Licensee: Sarah Travis. Registered Owner: R. Blezard, Brewer, Scotland Road.

Ropers Arms

Photographed in 1908 on the corner of St Oswald

Street and Percival Street and named after a former rope works which was situated nearby. This pub survived until the early 1970's before demolition.

Old Omnibus

At the junction of St Oswald Street and the former Salisbury Street, the pub's name derives from a coach service run by a former manager, Moses Dickinson, from the pub into the city centre (in competition with

James Hoult) Walk-up flats which, at the time of writing are in the process of demolition, were built over the site of this pub in the 1930's. Photographed in 1908 when the manager was James McCubbin. In 1939, another public house of the same name was built facing the original at the junction of St. Oswald Street and Maddocks Street which is still open to date.

Mitre

Listed at 78 St Oswald Street and clearly displaying the managers name when photographed c1900. Not listed in 1908, the site was later developed for walk-up flats which, at the time of writing, are being redeveloped.

Clock Inn

This pub, photographed in 1908 was on Hurst Street but was not listed in 1912. The premises were sold by Walkers in 1913.

1903 Licensee: Henry P. Speake Registered Owner: Burton, Bell & Co., Brewers, Wavertree

BH (left)

This old BH, photographed in the 1890's, stood in Hurst Street, off St Oswald Street.

Glass House Hotel

A major industry of Old Swan used to be glass-making. A large glass-works was built in 1825 at the summit of Edge Lane employing French craftsmen. The established trade, however, came to an abrupt end after a fraud trial in London resulted in the works closing down. The pub is the only reminder of a local

industry. The photograph is from 1926 when the current Glass House was in the course of construction with the old pub yet to be demolished. The present pub is listed at 45 Mill Lane at its junction with Cunningham Road.

St. George

This Green Lane pub, shown here in the 1920's, was destroyed in the War and has been replaced by

modern premises.

Travellers Rest

Located at the junction of Green Lane and Prescot Road. An old ramshackle structure photographed c1870. This would have been a stopping off point on the old Prescot Road turnpike. The large chimney formerly belonged to the Borax Works, which ran parallel to the houses shown on the left in Brookland

Road. The factory premises were replaced by Littlewoods Mail Order, which closed in 1983, and the site is currently a retirement home.

Corner Tavern

The Travellers Rest's replacement, the Green Lane

Tavern (since re-named the Corner Tavern), was built a little behind this site c1880. This view from 1996 shows the premises closed, with the former bus sheds now a supermarket.

Gardeners Arms

The Gardeners Arms was located on Broadgreen

GARDNERS ARMS c1920

TURKS HEAD 1908

Road on the old coaching route between Liverpool and Warrington. The photograph dates from the 1920's when the licensee was Annie Chester. Fair View Cottages adjoined the pub, so-named because they faced a huge nursery founded by George Cunningham in the late 18th century but now covered by roads and houses. The present structure, open to date, was built in the early 1930's.

1903 Licensee: Arthur James Kidd Registered Owner: Joseph Jones & Co. Brewers

Turks Head

Located in Knotty Ash (Liverpool 14) and on Prescot Road (re-named East Prescot Road in 1934, when the road was widened). Situated in the original Knotty Ash village on what is now the edge of Springfield Park. The Turks Head was the destination for the town's first omnibus service (c1833) initially operated by a Mr Bell and, from about 1840, by James Hoult. The horse-drawn buses ran from the pub to the Liverpool Town Hall, the journey taking about an hour and a half (due to the number of picking-up points including pubs and private roads of houses). Photographed in 1908, the pub closed in the 1920's.

Edge Lane, once the boundary of the Townships of West Derby and Wavertree, is an ancient highway and a former coaching route. Possibly older than Prescot Road, it was known to be used as a track for packhorses before roads were laid out between Liverpool and Prescot. Although Edge Lane is mainly in Liverpool 7, at its eastern end it becomes Liverpool 13.

BH

A number of cul-de-sacs stood off the part of Edge Lane now replaced by a huge shopping complex. One

of them was Douro Place on whose corner this pub was listed. Photographed in 1908 when the licensee was Thomas Middleton, it appears to have been run by the same family from the 1890's until the early 1950's as Thomas Middleton was listed until 1931 and from then Miss Ada Elizabeth Middleton. From the early 1950's, the pub was renamed the Crown Vaults until the early 1960's when the pub was rebuilt and renamed the Queen of Diamonds. In 1991, it was renamed the Travellers Rest, its current name.

BH

This was located at the junction of Edge Lane and

Tapley Place. Photographed in the 1890's when the licensee was Rebecca Clarke, the pub ceased trading as long ago as 1904. It was then listed as refreshment rooms until the 1930's and thereafter listed as a grocer's shop.

A large site between Edge Lane and Wavertree Road was formerly known as the Exhibition Ground,

HOULTS CORNER, OLD SWAN 1938

part of which was until recently a bus garage. A tournament hall on the site could accommodate some 15,000 people. In 1886, a new Exhibition Hall was opened on the site by Queen Victoria for the International Exhibition of Navigation, Commerce and Manufacturing. The same year, the Liverpool Shipperies Exhibition was held (probably an extension of the former). The following was written at the time concerning barmaids working at the Exhibition:

"It is popularly supposed in this enlightened country that Britons never can or will be slaves. This comforting belief, however, receives a shock upon learning the conditions upon which the barmaids at the exhibition occupy their position. For the paltry sum of about twelve shillings per week, these girls have to stand behind the bar from nine in the morning to about half past ten at night. All this without any relaxation whatsoever, and with scarcely any time to get a regular meal. Surely a system could be adopted by whereby they could have some little rest during the thirteen hours, and a definite time to get their meals. The hard lot of shop girls has often been commiserated; but here, without the pretence of necessity or custom that condemns shop girls to days of physical pain, the same barbarous regulation is enforced.

The espionage the girls are subjected to is something cruel. We generally boast that our English law always reckons a man innocent until proved guilty. Tom Sheen & Co. apparently take it for granted that all their employees are thieves. At any rate, if they do not, why do they have female searches, and who, if a girl is suspected, has the authority to search her? Why is poor old detective Allison continually trotting up and down the various rooms? Why is it that a man is constantly going to the various cash drawers and collecting the cash? And why is the officious Tom himself constantly haunting the rooms like a lost spirit? If he could only hear the uncomplimentary remarks that are made about him, even his complacency would, we fancy, be considerably ruffled. Our readers may probably not be aware that the barmaids have to give good references and a deposit of £5 for security. This ought to be sufficient guarantee for their good conduct. It is an insult to a respectable girl to undergo the indignity of being searched and watched as though she were a criminal of the deepest dye. The mayor is a kind hearted man and we trust he will do all in his power to make the life of these girls worth living."

Leaving the Edge Hill area for the Wavertree district (L15), the following were/are on Smithdown Road.

Royal Hotel

A large corner local, still trading on the corner of Smithdown Road and Langton Road. A highly decorative establishment both inside and out, the most

notable difference to the exterior of the pub today is the removal of the large Robert Cain sign displayed in this 1920's view when managed by John Clitherow. Probably rebuilt in the 1890's, prior to 1898 the pub was named the Angel.

Hatfield Hotel

Photographed in the 1920's on the corner of Crawford Avenue and Smithdown Road. Although a hotel, the premises were never licensed. Listed as Sefton Park Conservative Club by the 1950's, with the present club located behind the former hotel. The premises remain open as a different business.

SMITHDOWN ROAD, 1900

Willow Bank

An old 18th century former coaching inn, open to date. Set back a little off the main road, this view of the premises is from the 1920's when the manager was Robert Grail.

Brook House Hotel

A large, popular pub open to date. Photographed in the 1930's when the manager was James Yates. The original Brook House was built by Lord Sefton c1754, some 100 yards from the present pub (about the site of what is now Lidderdale Road). Probably named after an enclosed field in the vicinity called Brooklands. The premises were renamed the Finch & Firkin in 1994.

PICTON CLOCK, 1897

Waldeck

Open to date at the junction of Lawrence Road and Whitman Street, amongst a cluster of terraced streets that stand north of Smithdown Road and west of Wellington Road. This view is from the 1920's when the manager was John W. Little. A large mural of Liverpool's waterfront adorns the bar of the premises.

1892 Licensee: Joseph Brooks. Registered Owner: Burton, Bell & Co., Brewers, Wavertree.

Wellington

Open to date at the junction of Picton Road and Wellington Road. Picton Road is a major road, the continuation of Wavertree Road from Liverpool 7 through Liverpool 15. The view is from 1908 when the manager was John Kennedy. The building shown to the left of the pub on Picton Road (currently a furniture manufacturers) was originally a brewery named the Rose Brewery, belonging to Burton Bell

and Company Limited and taken over by Robert Cain in 1907.

The ancient Wavertree Village area still maintains its "village" identity. High Street, with 10 pubs originally, runs through the village where the following four pubs still trade.

Rose Vaults

The cottage adjoining the pub to the left has since been demolished and the site now landscaped. Mrs Annie Elizabeth Rushton managed the pub when it was photographed in 1908. After recent work to the

facade of the pub, where Lager is displayed in this photograph, it now reads Rose Vaults.

Thatched House

Before and after, the earlier photograph taken in 1908 contrasts dramatically with its later replacement.

Cock And Bottle

Listed as BH pre-1890's, the small section viewed to the right of the premises was once reputedly the smallest house in England. The former house was incorporated into the pub in the early 1950's.

Lamb Hotel.

Showing the pub shortly after the First World War, with an adjoining garage which reads: 'The Wavertree Motors and Carriages, late Dilworth. Open and Closed Carriages, Taxi Cabs for hire'. Dilworth was William F. Dilworth, listed in 1913 as omnibus and car proprietor, 109 High Street. The garage would have been in use as stables when the Lamb was a coaching inn in the 18th century. The former garage is now a beer garden.

1903 Licensee: William Mitchinson Registered Owner: Burton, Bell & Co., Brewers, Wavertree.

Coffee House Hotel

Open to date on Church Road North, close to High Street. The majority of lists name the premises simply as "Coffee House' with a few exceptions, including 1896, when it was listed as Wavertree Coffee House Commercial Hotel. A former coaching inn during the last century and a meeting place for local huntsmen, who would gather outside to go hunting in the countryside that then faced the pub. In common with other rural pubs, it may be of ancient date. A date of 1904 is displayed and it was probably rebuilt at that time since from the 1870's to cl904 the building was also a combined public house and brewery listed to Thomas Wright, brewer (Crown Brewery). This view from the 1920's shows Holman's Hairdressers occupying a portion of the building. By the 1930's, it became a sub-branch of Lloyd's Bank changing once again in the1950's to the Prudential Assurance, which remained until the 1960's when taken over by the pub.

Edinburgh Hotel

This view of Sandown Lane, off High Street, is from c1890. The Edinburgh, which is still trading, is the pub on the right. "Wavertree", the name partly displayed was probably referring to the brewers. When first licensed in the early 1860's, it was named

the Grapes, then the Victoria Hotel from 1865 until the pub took its current name c1880. The church shown in the distance was St. Mary's, Sandown Park (1850) which was destroyed during the war.

Aigburth & Garston

The following pubs were/are in L17 or L19.

Inglenook

A modern pub, photographed in 1974, still trading in Ullet Road

The Masonic Hotel

Still trading in Lark Lane. Extensive external alterations have taken place since this 1920's

photograph, when the licensee was William Henry Haigh. The segment displaying Walker's and the large number 34 have since been removed, as have the impressive railings.

Albert Hotel

Also trading to date in Lark Lane, the Albert is an elegant early Victorian public house built in the

1840's. There has been little external change since this photograph was taken in 1912.

Ye Old House At Home
and Travellers Rest

Both pubs were originally private houses adjacent to

each other in Aigburth Vale. Still trading, the 1950's photograph shows a former dairy fronting Ye Old House At Home with a passageway separating the two premises.

Travellers Rest

The 1971 photograph shows a new extension to replace the dairy whilst the original extension to Ye Old House At Home has been removed.

Aigburth Arms Hotel

Originally listed as the Crown in the early nineteenth century and located almost facing the Liverpool Cricket Club ground at 26-28 Aigburth Road (originally Park Lane). In the 1940's the road was widened and the number changed to 531. A

modern pub, the Kingsman, is now on the same site. During the last century, special horse-drawn buses ran between the pub and the Exchange, Dale Street, every Sunday. Brightly painted, they were actually lifeboats that had been mounted on wheels and drawn by four horses. The driver and conductor both dressed for the occasion wearing decorative "man-of-war" sailors' outfits. It was probably a lucrative marketing venture for the owners as the buses were nearly always full. The May 1898 photograph shows "trials of the heavy traffic motor vehicles" for use on the docks, organised by the Liverpool Branch of the Self-Propelled Traffic Association.

Cressington Hotel

Formerly listed as 6-8 Aigburth Road but changed to 577 during the 1940's. Located on the corner of Aigburth Road and Eslington Street (which still remains). The pub and its block were removed when

many members of the club realise it was once a pub. Named the Liverpool Arms until closure in the 1920's, it remained a licensed premises becoming the Market Members Club in the 1920's and 30's and the Woolton Road Social Club in the 1930's and 40's. It gained its current name in 1946. The premises were demolished in the 1970's when the present structure was built.

Swan

Open to date at the corner of James Street and Wood Street in Garston. There is little exterior

the road was widened in the 1960's. Photographed in 1905 when managed by Charles Clarke and the adjoining shop was Hanson's pharmacy. A proprietor in the 1920's was called the Admiral because he had been baptised Raleigh Frobisher Drake.

Garston Home Guard
Old Comrades Club

Open to date at 49 Woolton Road. I wonder how

difference to this 1920's photograph.

Volunteer Arms

The writing on the wall has survived and was revealed when the adjoining premises were demolished recently. A similar instance happened in Litherland when the demolition of a factory revealed a

large Threlfall's sign on the side of the Pacific in Linacre Road. Edward James Harrison was well known in the Garston areas trading as a carrier, beer seller and furniture remover between the 1860's and 1890's. The name of the pub is thought to be connected with the formation of a volunteer militia during the nineteenth century.

Blackburne Arms

Originally named the Cock and Trumpet from the 1850's to the 1950's when it became the Blackburne Arms. (Two other Liverpool pubs, on Cazneau Street and Whitechapel, were also called the Cock and Trumpet). The name Cock and Trumpet comes from the coat of arms of the Blackburn family, owners of the Manor of Garston although a trumpet is also used as a sign by Greenall Whitley (the word Cock in pub signs is of ancient usage, originating from the once popular sport of cock-fighting). Currently closed, the premises were renamed Dalys in the 1990's in an unsuccessful effort to stay open.

Canterbury Hotel

Standing at the corner of Window Lane and Canterbury Street. The pub is boarded up and shows

signs of fire damage when photographed in 1996. In 1903 the registered owner was Thomas Gregory, brewer of Gateacre.

Queens Hotel and Mona Castle

Photographed in 1953 when coronation flags still adorned the buildings. The view is of St Mary's Road

from Speke Road and features the Queens Hotel on the left and the Mona Castle on the right. The Queens Hotel still stands but the Mona Castle was demolished for structural reasons in the 1980's. Apparently the back of the pub was built on solid rock but the front on what had been a river bed.

Stanley Arms

The photograph shows a section of St Mary's Road in 1996. A date of 1863 and the initials JW (after John Williams, a butcher) are displayed on the front of the redbrick building. The arched entrance led into an abbatoir. The building on the left was the Stanley Arms, which closed in the 1920's, one of 13 pubs which once traded on the road.

Garston Hotel

At the beginning of the century, the pub had a tower on top which was referred to as the Lighthouse because it was used as a lookout for ships heading towards Garston Docks. The tower was removed and the facade rebuilt in its current style.

The Speke Estate (L24) was one of the most ambitious municipal projects of its kind. The City Council purchased 853 acres of agricultural land (nearly half of which was outside the city boundaries but later incorporated within Liverpool) with the intention of creating a comprehensive township. Work began in 1936, although the War halted progress. By 1957 over 6000 dwellings had been completed and amenities including a shopping centre, swimming pool, library and police and fire stations. Common with all the new council estates, pubs were built on the outskirts of the estate. As a result, Speke has possibly fewer pubs per head of population than any other area of Liverpool. The Pegasus and the Dove and Olive Branch are typical estate pubs.

Hunts Cross separates Speke from Woolton with two pubs trading to date: Hunts Cross Hotel and the Hillfoot (both photographed in 1971).

PEGASUS

DOVE AND OLIVE BRANCH

PALATINE HOTEL, GARSTON, WOOLTON ROAD, 1969.

ABOVE: THE HUNTS CROSS HOTEL, 1971

BELOW: HILLFOOT, 1971

Allerton & Childwall

ROSE OF MOSSLEY

The Rose of Mossley (L18) stands in Rose Lane (originally Mossley Vale) at its junction with Bridge Road in the Mossley Hill area of south Liverpool. The first photograph is from 1904 when the manager was Alexander Wood. During its early years it was named the Railway Inn, no doubt after the nearby railway station. The second view from 1925 when managed by Robert Shaw, states on the pubs facade proposals for the rebuilding of the Railway Inn with an accompanying picture of the new pub. Work had already commenced and a section of the old pub had already been demolished. On completion (c1930), the old name was changed to the present Rose Of Mossley.

During the 19th century Mossley Hill was amongst the most exclusive areas of Liverpool. Ship owners and merchants built impressive mansions and villas standing in their own grounds, many of which are still standing to-day. Adjacent to the pub are a group of early Victorian terraced houses named Stanley Terrace

and Gordon Place, somewhat out of place for the vicinity, that have survived and are now listed buildings. Similar property was once abundant in the older parts of Liverpool.

Childwall was for a long time more important than Liverpool. Childwall Parish embraced the townships of Thingwall, Much Woolton, Little Woolton, Garston, Allerton, Speke and Hale. Childwall Parish Church is probably the oldest surviving church in Liverpool, with 14th century and possibly Norman relics. Until the 1930's, it was open countryside, with only a few farms and large country houses. Once Childwall was absorbed into Liverpool in 1913, the character began to change and from the 1930's onwards, the fields and woodlands were rapidly replaced by housing estates. Nevertheless, the area around the church and Childwall Abbey Hotel (L16) on Score Lane still retains some of its previous character

Childwall Abbey Hotel

Photographed here in 1971, the building stands on the site of an even older pub and it is said that part of the wall of the hotel is a portion of the Chapel of St Thomas the Martyr, dating from 1484. The hotel was a favourite Sunday haunt, with large numbers of visitors arriving to play bowls and quoits in its gardens. Famous celebrities of the day, including actors Henry Irving and Ellen Terry and writer JM Barrie, inscribed their names with diamonds on the small window panes of the pub's Oak Room.

Half Way House

The 1946 illustration shows the pub on Woolton Road with the pumping tower for Dudlow Road

reservoir in the background.

Fiveways

The Fiveways (L16) is a post-war pub built on the site of a centuries old inn is on one of the major Queens Drive interchanges It has been recently revamped with a new facade.

Coronation

The Coronation (L16), photographed here in 1976, is a typical 1950's pub serving the extensive Childwall Valley Estate which extends along Childwall Valley Road from the end of Chelwood Avenue.

The Turtle

The Netherley Estate (L27) was an unmitigated disaster. Conceived in the 1960's, it was already an obsolete concept before construction started. Unfortunately, money had been allocated and the outrageous spine blocks and walk-throughs represented perhaps the last of the concrete 'build them high and never mind the quality' schemes to sneak through in this country. Within twenty five years the area had been levelled again. The Turtle, photographed here in 1982, represented all that was wrong with this kind of planning.

Woolton & Gateacre

Woolton (L25), is one of the oldest settlements in the Liverpool area. Evidence of an Iron Age camp has been found and Romans are said to have had a station on Camp Hill, although there is no evidence to support this. The Domesday book records Woolton as Uluentune from the Anglo Saxon Wulfa's tun (or Wulfa's homestead). The village remained relatively small with a population of only 439 in 1801. From then, Woolton began to expand rapidly, reaching a population of 2265 in 1841 and 4684 in 1871. Much of this growth was accounted for by the opening up of the quarry but there was also a need for labour in the docks and railway at Garston. In particular, there was an influx of Irish immigrants, especially in the Quarry Street area. Today it is difficult to imagine but Woolton had slum housing as bad as the inner city areas. In 1851, Rose Street had 58 houses with a total population of 445 occupants. Two houses, in Rodick Street and Rose Street had sixteen people sharing the same house.

As would be expected, beer houses proliferated, with many in the Quarry Street area. Drunkenness was such a problem that a new Police Station and Court Room were built on Quarry Street to contain the problem.

Today, Woolton retains its village character and is one of the most popular residential areas. For a 'village' of its size, it still retains a large number of pubs in relation to its population. On Quarry Street alone, there are five pubs still trading; more in one short street than the whole of Speke.

Coach & Horses

Open to date, on Woolton Street. In the 1908 photograph, the former stable is clearly visible. The adjoining cottage on the right was Lawton's plumbers

and printers. The other cottage was a private house.

The second photograph shows the modern replacement, renamed the Everglades in the 1980's before resuming its original name. The "out" building on the extreme right is all that remains of the old property.

Odd Fellows Arms

When I photographed this 19th century red sandstone building in 1996, a passer asked me why I was interested in it "Because it used to be a pub" I

replied. Looking at me in disbelief and laughing, he said "that's never been a pub and I've lived here all my life; it was a barber's once". It was, in fact, a pub named the Odd Fellows Arms, although now nearly beyond living memory (pre-1920's).

The Coffee House

The pub has a date stone 1641 and is the oldest pub in the village (and Liverpool). The photograph taken in 1971 shows a garage next door which has been replaced.

The Elephant

The Elephant, photographed here in 1983, has one of the most distinctive signs in Liverpool. A popular pub in Victorian times (as it is today), it advertised billiards, a bowling green and pleasure gardens in an 1889 advertisement when the proprietor was Thomas Stephenson.

The Hotel,

Private, Family and Commercial,

WOOLTON.

THOMAS W. STEPHENSON, Proprietor.

BILLIARDS.

BOWLING GREEN.

PLEASURE GARDENS.

CLUB & STOCK ROOMS.

LIVERY & BAIT STABLES.

Wines and Spirits of the Best Quality.

BASS' AND ALLSOPP'S ALES.

PIC-NICS, BALLS AND WEDDING PARTIES

WILL FIND EVERY ACCOMMODATION.

LOT 3.

54 VALE ROAD, WOOLTON
Liverpool

A shop and house with elevations of brick and stone with a slated roof. It contains:—

GROUND FLOOR: Shop, Two Entertaining Rooms, Kitchen, Back Kitchen, Larder, Bathroom.

FIRST FLOOR: Three Bedrooms, Boxroom.

ELECTRIC LIGHT, POWER & GAS.

OUTSIDE: Yard, Two W.C.'s, Coalplace, Toolshed.

The property is let at 23/- per week, making a total annual rent of £59 16s. 0d., the Landlord paying rates.

ASSESSMENT FOR RATES—£15 Net.

RATES 1947/8—£12 17s. 5d.

TENURE—Freehold and free from Chief Rent.

Further particulars from the Auctioneers:—

BOULT, SON & MAPLES, 5 COOK STREET, LIVERPOOL (Central 7487) *and at* 10 GRANGE ROAD, WEST KIRBY. (Hoylake 1763).

The Surveyors, EDMUND KIRBY & SONS, 5 COOK STREET, LIVERPOOL (Central 4377) *or*

The Solicitor, A. W. ROSS, 3 COOK STREET, LIVERPOOL (Central 8688).

NOTE.—While every care is taken in preparing these particulars, the rents, rates, and other calculations are not guaranteed and do not form any part of a contract for sale.

Wilmer Bros. & Co. Ltd., Printers, Birkenhead and Liverpool.

The Castle Hotel

The notice dates from 1948 when the property was up for auction. Located at the junction of Castle Street and Quarry Street, the property was originally the Castle Hotel when built in the 1840's. One of 18 pubs in the vicinity, its clientele was mainly men working the nearby Woolton Quarry which provided stone for the building of Liverpool Cathedral. Along with many other pubs in the early years of the century, the Castle fell victim to the 1904 Act which enabled magistrates to reduce the number of pubs in any given area as a means of controlling the epidemic of drunkenness that was sweeping the country at the time The property was converted into a private house in 1955.

COBDEN VAULTS, 1997

VICTORIA, 1997

ABOVE: GARDNERS, 1971

LEFT:
COUNTY COURT, 1997

Other pubs still trading in Woolton include the Victoria, County Court and Cobden Vaults all on Quarry Street and the Gardners in Vale Road.

Grapes Inn

Still trading at the corner of Allerton Road and Quarry Street in Woolton. The 1890's photograph advertises the pub as Importers & Bonders of Wines & Spirits with a bunch of grapes displayed on the Allerton Road facade.

FREDERICK AUSTIN,
LICENSED VICTUALLER,
Derby Arms Hotel.
162 & 164 ALLERTON ROAD
WOOLTON.

Wines and Spirits of the Choicest Quality.

W. B. ASHTON

GRAPES INN

TOP: BROWN COW, 1963   **ABOVE: BEAR & STAFF**
LEFT: GATEACRE HALL, 1976
BELOW: BLACK BULL, 1976

Gateacre has four pubs still trading in the village: Black Bull; Brown Cow; Bear and Staff; Gateacre Hall Hotel.